First Facts™

Learning about Money

Checks, Credit, and Debit Cards

by Roberta Basel

Consultant:
Sharon M. Danes, PhD
Professor and Family Economist
University of Minnesota

Capstone press

Mankato, Minnesota

First Facts is published by Capstone Press,
151 Good Counsel Drive, P.O. Box 669, Mankato, Minnesota 56002.
www.capstonepress.com

Library of Congress Cataloging-in-Publication Data
Basel, Roberta.
    Checks, credit, and debit cards / by Roberta Basel.
    p. cm. — (First facts. Learning about money)
    Summary: "Introduces the reader to payment methods, including checks, debit cards, and
credit cards. Includes an activity and fun facts"—Provided by publisher.
    Includes bibliographical references and index.
    ISBN-13: 978-0-7368-5394-1 (hardcover)
    ISBN-10: 0-7368-5394-4 (hardcover)
    1. Money—Juvenile literature. 2. Checks—Juvenile literature. 3. Credit cards—Juvenile
literature. 4. Debit cards—Juvenile literature. I. Title. II. Series.
HG221.5.B294 2006
332.1'7—dc22   2005023096

Editorial Credits
Wendy Dieker, editor; Jennifer Bergstrom, set designer; Bobbi J. Dey, book designer;
    Scott Thoms, illustrator; Jo Miller, photo researcher/photo editor

Photo Credits
Capstone Press/Karon Dubke, cover, 5, 6, 7, 14–15, 17, 21
Corbis/Dan Lamont, 20; Ephraim Ben-Shimon, 13; Joe McBride, 8–9; Simon Marcus, 18–19
Getty Images Inc./Taxi/S. Shipman, 12

1 2 3 4 5 6 11 10 09 08 07 06

Table of Contents

Paying Without Cash

The last time you went shopping, did you see people buying things with plastic cards instead of using cash? Or maybe they wrote **checks**. Many people today often pay without cash.

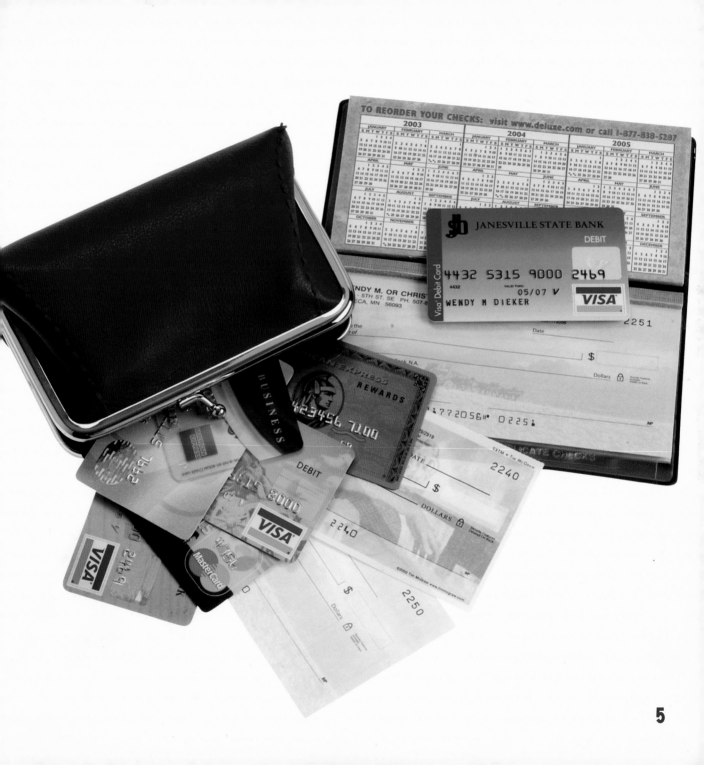

Checks

Checks let people spend money in their bank **accounts**. Checks tell the bank to pay someone. Money is taken from the check writer's account.

JAMES C. MORRISON
MARY A. MORRISON
1765 SHERIDAN DRIVE
YOUR CITY, STATE   01002

342

DATE

PAY TO
THE ORDER OF

$

DOLLARS

Security Features
Included.
Details on Back.

JANESVILLE STATE BANK
201 N. MAIN ST.
P.O. BOX 369
JANESVILLE, MN 56048-0369
507-234-5108

MEMO

MP

⑆091903242⑆ 000⑈000⑉

© DELUXE WALLET OR DUPLICATE

SPECIALTY BLUE

Mrs. Thom writes Ryan a check for washing her car. He takes it to the bank. The bank takes money from Mrs. Thom's account and gives it to Ryan.

Debit Cards

A **debit card** works like a check, but without paper. Mike uses his debit card to buy a snowboard. The store's computer reads the card. It sends a message to his bank. The bank moves money from Mike's checking account into the store's account.

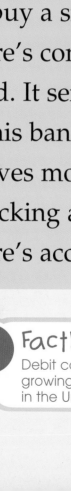 **Fact!**
Debit cards are the fastest growing form of payment in the United States.

online banking

Valley Bank

Credit Card

Download Print

Select Account

My Credit Card ▼

Account Summary

Account Nickname	Visa Classic
Account Number	4546-xxxx-xxxx-0123

Total Credit Line	$1,000.00
Credit Used (Debt)	– $300.00
Credit Left to Use	$700.00

Account Activity

Date	Description	Amount
10 July 06	Mega-Mart	$50.00
13 July 06	Clothes Connection	$120.00
20 July 06	Hank's Foods	$85.00
21 July 06	The Art Store	$45.00
	Total Debt	$300.00

Valley Bank

134 Main Street
Anytown, MN 12345
(123) 456-7890
info@valleybank.com

10

Credit and Debt

With checks and debit cards, people buy things with money they already have. But people can also borrow money to buy things. They pay back borrowed money later.

The amount of money a person can borrow is called a **credit** line. The money a person has to pay back is called **debt**.

! Fact!
About 18 percent of purchases for items such as clothes and groceries are made with credit cards.

Credit Cards

Credit cards let people use their credit. Emily uses her credit card to buy clothes. The credit card company pays the store.

Later, the credit card company sends Emily a bill for everything she bought. She pays back her debt by sending a check to the credit card company.

Interest

    Credit card companies let people choose how quickly they pay off their debt. Some people pay off the whole amount at once.

Debt
$10.00

+

Interest
$0.57

Others pay only a little at a time. Making small payments costs extra money. A small fee, or **interest**, is added to debt that is not paid off right away.

Total Amount to Pay
$10.57

Growing Debt

Debt grows when it is not paid off quickly. More interest is added for each month that the debt isn't paid off. Items that don't cost very much can end up costing a lot more money as interest adds up.

! Fact!
Only 40 percent of Americans pay off their credit card debt each month.

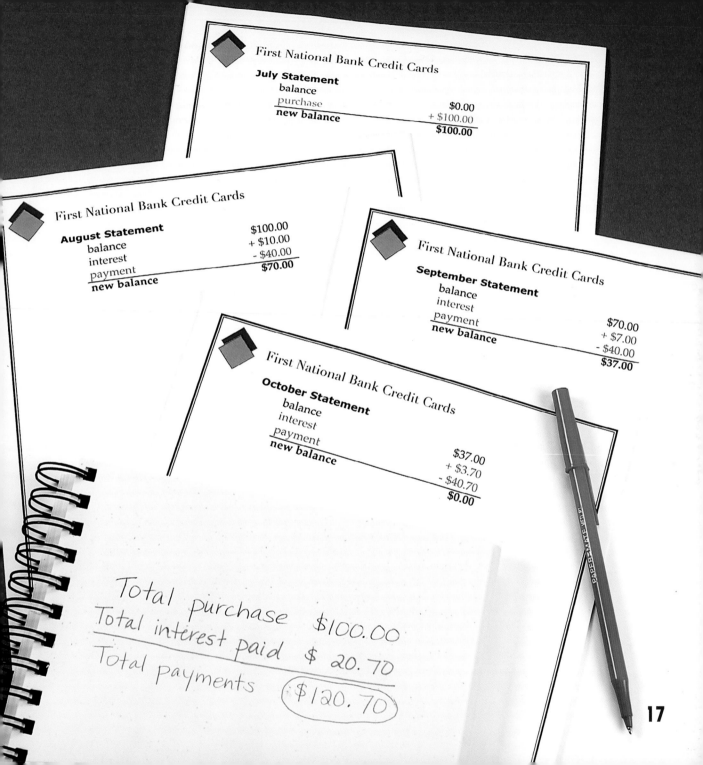

First National Bank Credit Cards

July Statement
balance
purchase $0.00
new balance   + $100.00
             $100.00

First National Bank Credit Cards

August Statement $100.00
balance   + $10.00
interest   - $40.00
payment   **$70.00**
new balance

First National Bank Credit Cards

September Statement
balance
interest $70.00
payment   + $7.00
new balance   - $40.00
           $37.00

First National Bank Credit Cards

October Statement
balance
interest
payment
new balance $37.00
        + $3.70
        - $40.70
        $0.00

Total purchase $100.00
Total interest paid $ 20.70
Total payments $120.70

Be a Wise Spender

Wise spenders use their checking accounts and credit carefully. They don't spend more money than they have in their checking accounts. Wise spenders only use credit when they can pay it back quickly.

Fact!

More purchases are made with credit and debit cards than with checks.

Soon, people will not need their checks or credit cards with them when they shop. They will need only their fingers! In 2004, Pay By Touch introduced a machine that lets people use their fingerprints to pay for the things they buy. Each customer's fingerprint is connected to their checking account or credit card.

Hands On: Write a Check

You can learn how to write a pretend check. Trace a copy of the check on page 6 to get started.

What You Need

copy of the check on page 6
pen

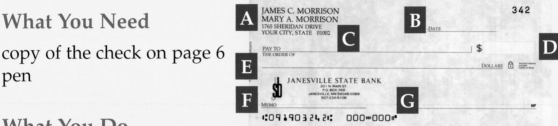

What You Do

1. Look at the place labeled A. Write your name and address there. On real checks, this will already be printed.
2. On the line labeled B, write today's date.
3. Pretend you are buying something at a store. Write the store's name on the line labeled C.
4. How much money are you pretending to spend? Write the numbers in box D.
5. On line E, write the words of the numbers from box D.
6. You can write a little note, or memo, about what you are pretending to buy on line F.
7. Now sign your pretend check. Sign your name on line G.

People can write checks only for the amount of money they have in their checking accounts. The bank won't pay the store if there isn't money in the account.

Glossary

account (uh-KOUNT)—an agreement to keep money in a bank, as in a checking or savings account

check (CHEK)—a piece of paper used to tell the bank to pay money from an account

credit (KRED-it)—the amount of money a person can borrow

credit card (KRED-it KARD)—a card used to borrow money to buy things

debit card (DEB-it KARD)—a card that lets a person use the money from a bank account

debt (DET)—the amount of money that a person owes

interest (IN-trist)—a small fee added to debt that isn't paid off

Read More

Cooper, Jason. *Paying without Money.* Money Power. Vero Beach, Fla.: Rourke, 2003.

Hall, Margaret. *Credit Cards and Checks.* Earning, Saving, Spending. Chicago: Heinemann Library, 2000.

Loewen, Nancy. *Cash, Credit Cards, or Checks: A Book about Payment Methods.* Money Matters. Minneapolis: Picture Window Books, 2005.

Internet Sites

FactHound offers a safe, fun way to find Internet sites related to this book. All of the sites on FactHound have been researched by our staff.

Here's how:
1. Visit *www.facthound.com*
2. Type in this special code **0736853944** for age-appropriate sites. Or enter a search word related to this book for a more general search.
3. Click on the **Fetch It** button.

FactHound will fetch the best sites for you!

Index